After Midnight

Also by Joseph N. Manfredo:

Only The Living
(A Memoir)

After Midnight

Poems and Pontifications

Joseph N. Manfredo

Order this book online at www.trafford.com
or email orders@trafford.com

Most Trafford titles are also available at major online book retailers.

Printed in the United States of America.

ISBN: 978-1-4269-3620-3 (sc)

ISBN: 978-1-4269-3621-0 (hc)

ISBN: 978-1-4269-3622-7 (e-book)

Library of Congress Control Number: 2010909189

*Our mission is to efficiently provide the world's finest, most comprehensive book publishing
service, enabling every author to experience success. To find out how to publish your
book, your way, and have it available worldwide, visit us online at www.trafford.com*

Trafford rev. 07/27/2010

 www.trafford.com

North America & international
toll-free: 1 888 232 4444 (USA & Canada)
phone: 250 383 6864 ♦ fax: 812 355 4082

To those
who touched my life,
and changed it,
for better
or worse,
forever.

EPIGRAPH

"Poetry doesn't belong to those who write it, but those who need it."
Mario Ruoppolo to Pablo Neruda in the movie "Il Postino."

"...the difference between prose and poetry is that in prose all lines in a paragraph except the last one go clear out to the margin."

Jeremy Bentham

PREFACE

These works, created over a span of sixty years, won interest from family and a few friends who encouraged me to publish. Perhaps the reader will find at least one composition of sufficient merit to save the book from the dust bin in which case the effort will have been worthwhile.

Contents

The Early Years

Wonderment

1951 - 1956

The young man was far away from home for the first time and feeling lonely. He sat in the dark, alone, in a small, rented room high above the city streets below. A bright moon floated in a star studded sky outside his window. By its light he could see the desk top and the clock which showed it to be a little after midnight. He thought about her and of home and, bathed in moonlight, he began to write his feelings.

The next morning he arose, noted the scrap of paper on the desk, read it again and decided to keep it. He penciled a title above it then carefully placed it in the desk drawer.

He called it, "After Midnight."

After Midnight

To whom can I write, for my spirit is troubled?

With whom can I speak --- for lonely I be?

My thoughts, seeking comfort, would find that far lover

Whose mind struck with mine such a sweet euphony.

Neither rhyme nor reason exists for this theme

Conceived and brought forth by emotions regime.

Yet, peace there is none---as there's no one to share---

Or to lend complete solace by saying,....

"I care..."

One darkening evening, while day dreaming, I heard, then saw a military jet plane flying high over the tall church spires which reached toward the heavens, just outside my window, and wondered what lay beyond, and what purpose my life was meant to serve.

The Definition

Up in the unnamed blue of the sky – the roar
Of a thunderjet – sailing by.
Surely in this war birds cry
Some words of my definition lie.

See those monsters bending low,
Cringing neither from rain nor snow,
Casting shadows on roofs below?

Out beyond that useless pale,
Pasted 'gainst a blackening veil,
The words of my definition sulk,
Intact – untouched – in some fair dale.

Someday, I'll journey out there too.
I'll vault the spires which block my view,
And leaving terra far behind
Strike out, for trails strange and new.

Then when these spires are only dots
And planes just streaks on a distant shore,
I'll gaze upon my fancied thoughts,
Too distant even for birds of war.

And then .... perhaps .... I'll really know,
For then,.... perhaps ... at last I'll find
The arrow for my pensive bow.....
That phrase.... which now eludes my mind.

Childhood dreams, hopes and aspirations grow distant as we
move out into the world.
We begin to glimpse that life's destiny may not be what we
innocently pictured it to be.
Yet we press on.
What is this motivation that keeps us going, almost blindly,
toward an unknown future?
Is it a life force?
A spiritual predestination?
Or something else?

Whence Comes The Stirring?

What prompts a man to toil on when
all life's purposes seem gone,

When his ideals, once seen so clear,

Have fled from sight with yester's dawn?

Why does he plod, from day to day

Like birds that fly an uncharted way?

Whence comes the stirring within his breast

Which never seems to let him rest

'Till comes that time, which comes to all,

When from this earth-know life we fall?

Can it be, as some would say, that
man conforms to one above,

That each man's breast contains a soul.....

Inspired through life by His great love?

Message of The Bells

Church bells call out
in the dark winter evening.
I listen,
alone,
in a room,
above the snow covered city.
Street lights wear snowflake halos
down there,
way down there,
where cars and people
seem so small.
Are the bells celebrating
a historical event?
Or something that is
happening now,
tonight,
as it does,
this time
every year?

Inspiration

Pealing, vibrant---chanting Holy Anthems,

Church bells, just outside the window swing,

Sending upward on wings of love

The echoing choruses all peoples sing.

Inspiration born upon a day of a long ago year---

and yet so near.

For listen to the bells and say,

"My Father was born on a long ago day."

But nay -- for something –

be it the bells conceiving inspiration—

To the soul a secret tells,....

"Tonight it is and always was.

 He is born again..."

In the lilting voice...

of the Christmas Bells.

Desk Top

Messy desk before me sits
Cluttered like my mind.
Wish that I might
Clear my wits
As easily as thine.

Radio, ink, pencils, scrap,
Letters, glasses, books and trap.
Love and hate,
Thoughts and fears,
Joy and sorrow,
Longing,
Tears.

One as complex as the other.
One I'll fix –
And one I'll mother.

Indecision

With all the times the sun has dawned,

so faithfully, so true,

With every morn I wonder if

tomorrow will dawn, too.

And yet, I know, through countless years,

to rise the sun's not failed,

But knowledge of the past does not

the future's dreams unveil.

So, despite the ageless, patterned weave

that life, I've heard, entails,

I cannot help but wonder where

lifes course tomorrow sails.

Universities offering a co-operative education program allow the student to alternate between several months of full time school followed by several months of work each semester.

The blessing of this system is that during work periods the student is paid, thus earning tuition, while, at the same time, gaining hands-on experience using what is being learned at school.

The curse of this system is that students, whose work sites are far removed from the school, are constantly interrupting any emotional relationships formed at either venue. Time is always too short.

Hence: "Time."

Time

Element of elements, master of my peace.
Lord of childish mans attempt your
rampant pace to cease.

Why? oh why? cannot my love and
I find blessed pleasure
Within a portion of your soul—
a segment of your measure?

Is there a way – mysterious, whereby, by concentration,
Two people, very much in love,
might captivate duration?

Or can unpleasant moments of disdainful separation,
By the same exotic means be thinned
to bits of hesitation?

Come, tell me, master of my fate,
swift changing overlord,
Why do you sometimes savor sweet
and sometimes, taste abhorred?

How can you shine a blessing, for short
months of unchained bliss,
Then swiftly, with retracting hand,
steal off with my loves kiss?

Yet, you are not invincible, to reign till we both die!
For we will one day make you slave
to my sweet love and I.

And we'll be kinder masters than you have been in past,
For in your presence love will live,
And we shall make you last.

The fraternity pledge endures several months of hazing from fraternity members. During the final week, dubbed "Hell Week," he is deprived of sleep. After school, supper and homework are completed he is given a list of chores to work on during the night. If caught sleeping he is punished and threatened with expulsion. Members of all fraternities at the school are obliged to keep all pledges awake during classes. Each pledge wears a large, hand-made sign, on a string necklace, which identifies the fraternity he is pledging.

I was the dreaded, "hard nose" fraternity member sitting behind this poor Hell Week pledge during a metallurgy class.

Hell Week Pledge

The boy before me is a pledge whose
soul right now is lost.
See there the wrinkled, worried brow
– so taut, so tempest tossed?

His mind, right now, a mixture of
remorse, disgust and hate
For the vicious, scheming members in
whose hands doth rest his fate.

See him now ... his head it tumbles,
from his palm where it did rest.
For a moment he sleeps soundly,
with his chin upon his chest.

Ah! but not for long this pleasure –
not for long this blest repose.
Just a touch, a whispered warning –
see the nervous twitch of nose?

Up it snaps, his head is giddy ...
blinking eyes his thoughts do tell,
"If this 'hard nose' thinks it's funny ...
to this pledge it's just plain hell!"

Life surprises us with its' transient behavior.
What seems permanent can disappear in the blink of an eye.
It begs the question "Is there something more eternal?"

Somewhere, A Staff

When man learns, by the healing of many wounds,

That all he loves, all he wants — all
that his bosom hopes for

Is not for him—can never be, for long, in his possession,

When this he has learned: To relish all he has,

For soon, quicker than the approach of sudden thunder,

It will be gone—exchanged by life's course
for a newer, stranger circumstance;

When this he sees as surely as he sees the
sun burning in a noonday sky,--

Then he has arrived beyond the reach of vain beliefs,--

Then he is ready to seek a higher thing….an
afterlife... a staff of promise upon which to lean.

Surely, in that moment he must know that
One there be, whose mercy far outreaches
humanity's yearnings and its richest dreams,

And there a respite lies, awaiting, unperturbed
through centuries, the searching of his soul.

1st Hour P.M. was written during a Metallurgy class scheduled for the first hour after lunch at Kettering University, previously known as General Motors Institute.

The author, suffering from boredom and a heavy meal, was moved to put down on paper what many of his classmates felt regarding this exceedingly dull instructor.

1ˢᵗ Hour PM

He sits and taps the table top,
With chalk, as he does talk.
I wonder if he knows that I would rather take a walk,
Ignoring all he stands for,....Metallurgy makes be balk!

I sometimes wish I had the nerve
To tell him, "Mr. B.,
Tell your story to the birds!
It really doesn't interest me!"

But neither will I speak this,
Nor will he tell the birds.
So I'll go on ignoring,
With an average of two thirds.

And while others notes are taking,
Plugging hard to hit this course,
I'll compose, for so they call this,
'til that dry instructor's hoarse!

And if he won't quit 'fore I do,
You can bet this jewel will last
From the first words that he utters,
To the end of every class.

Strong emotions are remembered, sometimes,
as I sit, quietly, peacefully, at rest.
Powerful feelings build until they overflow
onto paper....and a poem is born.

Heaven Will Miss You

Heaven will miss you while you are away
down here with me.....
Pacing time on miles of soil and sorrow called Earth.
Hazy glimpses of reality beckon to my heart -
I reach to the skies and grasp your yielding form.
With trembling arms enfolding I draw my destiny
to earth – to my bosom...

Breath a fierce vow to match my passion.
Crinkled lips to face the jubilant onslaught of mine...
Stardust hair to clutch in eager fingertips
While smoldering green eyes spread conflagration
o'er combustible brown.

Touch my cheek – see how warm – how flushed with desire...
Play your game of taunting invitation,
and play it well.
I live but once – and plan a place in memory
only for the love I've never conquered.

While Spring breathes a quickened pace into the heart –
While Summer blooms a world of fitful lovers lanes –
While Fall announces tender moments with every falling leaf –
While Winter tightens corded muscles of resistance,
to drive Love indoors –

'Til these Seasons circumvent the globe on
which you've come to live
I'll test each day to see if maybe this one- maybe today –
your tempting bosom may be my resting place.

One day you'll be acquiescent – and I
shall dwell in the depths
of the passions
of a Goddess.

"Every man is a poet when he is in love."
Plato

My Love

In numerous places have I sought my love –
Dreams, awake and sleeping.
I knew her once – warm, alive – so real.
We laughed then at her bantering squelch
Of my arduous attempts, little knowing
How soon was the chasm ahead
How long and often the heartache of remembrance.

With youth-like simplicity we accepted our pleasant bliss,
As a babe the delicacy of his Mother's breast…
as something of eternal nature,
Never realizing what treasures we held then,
So easily, so lightheartedly.
Ours was the world and all its glories.

Oh! For the time I kissed her first-
Delicately- as if the fragrant petals were of fine honeycomb,
Did I touch her lips-
Yielding to mine ever so slightly.

With this holy conception did our love begin –
a sight – a word – a kiss –
A promise of return.
It was nourished, unseen by us,
until a budding awareness of each other's hearts appeared.

As any precious thing it grew with tender care
A touch of intimacy only in the meeting of our eyes.

The times of separation have been cruel,
The master teacher, Life, has taken her
away and brought her back again
As a wave rushes to caress a shore only
to slip out of sight once more.

Once more I see her close
I tremble with love, with desire
With fear.
I pray she will stay,
And in her eyes I see an image of my thoughts.

God grant us this....
Give to us the embers of a never-dying flame
And let it thrive again,
For should she leave once more
my soul, so ravaged now
Would surely find its compensation in the arms
Of spiritual death.

My Praise

I laugh, I sneer, I shout and sing –
And challenge all that life may bring
My way.

I laugh because the past is scarred o'er now.
I sneer because they fall before my wicked vow.
I shout that all may know
My confidence 'gainst all the follies life can hold.
I sing the song of sweet lipped vengeance
and it's sting.

Life is a garden filled with
All the flowers 'neath the sun......
I walk and pick,
at will,
The fairest blooms
One....
by.....
one.

"Trust, like the soul, never returns, once it is gone."
Publius Syrus: *Maxims*

She Lied

Oh' me...again the eternal error.
A falsehood is a falsehood.
There are lies and there are lies...
And these latter puncture me,
Still, no pain.

Lessons become less toilsome as
They progress,
The work and heartache remains
experienced.
However, more satisfaction arises
From the knowledge gained at each
To balance chagrin and disappointment.

I thank you for having lied to me.
Your move has restored to equilibrium
The tender scales of a neophyte mind.
I thought, for just a while, that
Trust of female had returned

.

With master stroke of feigned
Innocence the dream became still born,
And I am twist again

.

For constructive, punitive measure
I thank you, little girl.
Once more I look upon this sea
And smile the salty smile of years
Before the mast –
Still amazed at
All the fish before me.

"Time shall unfold what plaited cunning hides."
Shakespeare: King Lear I.i.

Time Stands Still

Where has youth gone?
The hope and expectations that once were mine
No longer touch a spark within.
Time stands still....

And endless seconds swiftly melt
Together into passing years.
I remember well – her smile and her charms.
Oh! This was happiness, too!
This was youth.
A pounding heart and racing pulse
Cold nights – a kiss exchanged beneath
The web of falling snow
And sparkling street lamps.
"You're crazy – but I love you that way!"
Time stands still.

Back flood the fragments that awake old senses.
The cool green grass of "our hill"
Beneath us – shaded by the black canopy of night –
And love so clean
And fresh.

I loved her not, and this she knew.
But, she was all a man could want..
Devotion, wit, desiring more than all else
To please this boy she loved.
Time stands still....

Yes! Yes! Remember how she cried
Each time you left for home?
Real tears – warm, salted with sorrow –
And you know their taste as passionate kisses of farewell

Transferred their burning path to your cheek
And the clock....tick, tock, tick tock,
Slowly, stolidly marking off the lease you held on happiness....
And didn't it always strike the hour early?

Its bell warned lovers of the coming desk clerk,
Who smiled and said, "It's time to go."

Remember giggles – oh! And sour notes she quailed
When blended voices spoke of parties or church nights.
She tried – and you feigned admiration for this queer ability
To disguise the simplest tune.
Yet – Time stands still...

No more her laugh and dancing eyes.
No tears so sweet to wet your lips
No pangs of anticipation
No impulses to hold her close because
She is so cute in her own, childish way.
Her malformed fingers no longer to caress your hair.
Her tiny form no longer priming
Your emotions as she comes walking down the street.

With all the bloodshed of a falling Caesar
Your heart beheld the knife of betrayal
With which she rent your soul.
Time stands still...

For youth was lost in this vicinity
And hope and expectations no longer
Touch a spark within.

Where...where has my youth, my own youth gone?

Now, time stands still.

To The College Boy

Softly, tread softly now,
Short ahead, beyond the yawning
rocks, is light.
Softly, - softly now – Oh tender
youth.
Yours is life and years of time,
Much pathway to find – and no
need for haste.
Softly, oh softly…now you grow,
now you form –
Retain what youth you hold,
intact,
For just beyond is life and
minutes – yea! Years of time
To recklessly exhaust your
hoard of energies.
And all you selfishly hold back now,
while learning,
May later be released to bring
A richer happiness.
Softly, - tread softly now,
Oh child of green years.
Tomorrow after tomorrow are
Yours – all yours.

"How soon hath Time, the subtle thief of youth,
Stol'n on his wing my three-and-twentieth year."
John Milton: *On His Having Arrived at the Age of Twenty-three.*

Upon Becoming Twenty-Two

I wonder why it is?
I never feel my age, as such.....
'Tis Madness – but a child is me –
Silly pretense... that I am a man.
Sillier that some believe
by seeing accomplishments made.
Know they not that a daring child
May outperform the wisely wary adult?
It's true.
Just look – behold the man.
Babes' face, with bitter cynicism
Just beyond.
At twenty two a child is me – aged
By errors, yes, yet...
Holding to those childish
Dreams that all will soon be well,
That peace will come,
That debts will go,
That life will last and blessings grow.
How juvenile – a child is me.
Yet, think!
Next year I'm twenty three.

During the final two months of our last college year a group of us rented a small cabin on the shores of Lake Fenton, Michigan, several miles from campus. Each day we car pooled to and from school. We ate daytime meals at the fraternity house. Evenings and weekends, with homework completed, we swam and took turns water skiing, pulled by our neighbors boat. He was a high ranking official with the United Auto Workers, vacationing with his wife and little daughter. The daughter and I found we had kindred spirits. We sat on the dock sometimes, feet dangling in the water, and talked. On the last day of summer, as her parents loaded the car, she gave me a hug and kissed my cheek goodbye.

Her name was Linda.

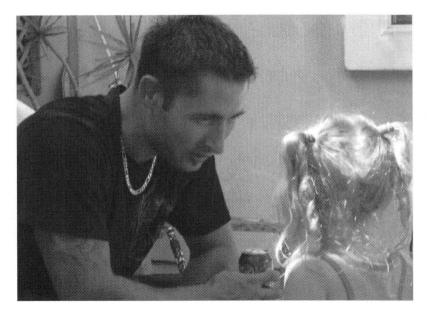

"Am I the nicest girl you ever met?"

To Linda

How I quaked with pride
When you asked,
"Am I the nicest girl you ever met?"
Your eyes of blue innocence
Pierced my soul
And taught an eternal lesson.
In your rosy smile I felt
Again, a warmth of love,
And your sincerity will ever leave
The scar of past hurt enclosed
With new hope
Of happy times to come.

Yes! Oh, Yes!
You were the nicest girl I'd ever met,
And nicest still.
I could not tell you more just then,
How you lifted all the broken dreams,
And melted them together –
Nor how the throbbing heart of mine
Spoke a wish of having
One like you, someday.

These things you gave I cherish always,
And in my moments of thoughtful
Reminiscence, I see your face,
Tenderly soft,
Yet strong of future prospects.

A long, long time from now
I'll swift recall
How, with my heart
Your laughter
And your kiss
Played tricks,
And all this,
Even more,
From just a child
Of six.

Bravado often masks the fear of pain.

Hobby

Hold me,
Fondle me,
Feel of my might!

Love me
While you may
Just for tonight!

You are the one,
You are
The selection.

The latest seduction
In my vast,
Choice,
Collection!

Sometimes a few words, well chosen, can speak volumes.

In Short

Sand,
Sprinkled lightly
By the wind –
Beaten crudely
By the sea -
Tread upon
By countless feet -
Then
Worn to dust
By time -
That's me.

We live in a three dimensional world.
Except for love.
It has more.

Boundaries

Love hath no beginning
I knew her in my dreams.

Love hath no limits
She partakes in all my schemes.

Love hath no cellar
My love is deep in essence.

Love hath no ceiling
My Heaven is her presence.

Love hath no timing
She leaves my memory never.

Love hath no ending.
God hath given us forever.

Life

A balance of
Unfulfilled dreams
And
Unexpected happiness.

To Her

A broken arm will mend
with time
and proper care.
A broken heart will, too…
If you are there.

To Education

Come to me
Caress me
Jostle my countenance
Change my ways.
And when you go forever
Leave a memory
Of my youthful days.

Bella Mia

Bella Mia – my pretty,
you'll always be.
Cara Mia – beloved,
You are to me.

Your smile, your kiss,
Your joy, your sorrow
Will linger as guides
in my life's tomorrow.

The hand that held mine
Is like unto no other.
My own "Bella Mia."
My own,
my Mother.

We scribble a thought – an idea – from time to time. Years later we find them. Each one stands alone, unconnected to the others. They seem innocuous yet, in love with one's own words, one is reluctant to toss them away. They are random. Call them random thoughts.

Random Thoughts

ΩΩ

Perhaps we are doomed to live our greatest moments completely unaware of their import, until they have gone by, because of our tendency to look to tomorrow for the apex in all things. Am I missing today's "great moment?"

ΩΩ

The virtue so earnestly sought by man in woman is often found, sometimes as a real condition, sometimes imagined. The ability to recognize the difference is rare.

ΩΩ

If we spend more time rushing to save time than putting it to useful purpose its passage may accelerate with less result. Sometimes plodding is faster.

ΩΩ

Non-conformism weighs heavily on the minds of some, driving them to imitate one another in being different, thus losing the meaning of non-conformism. When we are all identically different from the norm we become the new norm.

ΩΩ

Progress is the dividend of invested time.

"But I'm not so think as you drunk I am."
  J. C. Squire: *Ballade of Soporific Absorption.*

The Results of a Hot Dog & Beer at 11:00 PM

To bed, to bed, the hours come together
Like husband and wife on romantic nights.
Stars sail 'cross a darkish sky.
People cease their living pace,
And, one by one, creep into slumbers might.
Quiet grows this place, whilst auto
Horns dim down to far-off echoes.
To bed, to bed – the witching hour approaches.
To bed, tis time for sleep,-
Your eyes repent the ache of this days vent.
To bed, to sleep, let slumber steal your toil
And bury all, 'til morn doth come,
Beneath its' fluffy soil
To bed – dear soul – to bed.

You & I

When you and I knew scarce a thing about the future
And all was rosy red with skies of blue above,
How sweet t'was then to hold in mine your dainty hand
How pleasant just to lie and speak to you of love.

A home, both new and owned by us
A yard with grass and trees
A fence with pickets and a rust-hinged gate
French window which would open to the breeze
A dog for child's companion and for guardian
A room of books on rows and rows of shelves
A fireplace with a blonde fur rug-piece
Upon whose hearth, by night, would dance our elves.

All these and more to you and ours I promised
It made our hearts beat fast to picture it.
Remember – three children; two
for you and two for me,
a boy, a girl, and two heads on the
last would make it three.
and then we'd laugh a bit.

Sweet-lipped beauty gone away – and
sad to say – I do know where,
Into warm arms, not mine.
Our ways have split – and still I would be there.
Still would I laugh and frown, mock
anger when you teased,
Still would I feel the painful joy of
being laughed at by my love,
when e're she pleased.

All this and more to you and I was given.
Your smiles and tears came with mine each time.
Remember the first touch of lips?
Said I, "So warm, so alive, so real."

Your mocking retort said "Would you
rather I were cold and dead?"
My sincerity was quashed,
but your dancing eyes and smile set all aright again.
From that moment on was I yours
to love, to mock, to beckon,
to put to flight.

Alas, my peach of pink curvature – who
cuddles now the softness I but tasted
Nay – sampled but its fragrance?

So many, many ghosts – to think of
them brings rest, of a kind,
for it requires effort not to relive the past,
and only by yielding to post images
can my mind cease turmoil
Yet, yet to write them is a challenge.

How does one describe the smell of
rain on spring-tufted lawns?
What can express the fair and fine figure
of a girl in white shorts midst the park
swings, pushing a tiny sister to and fro?
And know you what my thought then was?
"That is what I've sought and seen in all my dreams."

Yet you were, then, inaccessible.
How could I dare hope that the sight
which caused a minor miracle in my heart
would one day be, but briefly, mine?
And tennis, another time.
It was a friend and I who pretended
knowledge of the sport
while you and your friend played at
missing in the next court.
We borrowed your tennis ball, for we had none....
And then the greatest event of the summer occurred.....

for I returned the ball to you, as you sat on the swing,
moving gently toward and away from me.

Recall, you invited my toss, which
you missed – and then -
I retrieved it – placed it in your hand, slowly, gently,
relishing the warmth and nervous moisture
of your silk-smooth palm and delicate fingers.

So significant, that momentary touch,
the symbol of all we would have.....

We were given so much, for such a short time.
The very richness of our gifts choked off our having.....
just as the richness of some foods,
in small quantity, destroys the appetite.

And carelessly the dish of happiness was
brushed aside in bitter quarrel.....

I have oft in elegance dined since.
Still, the tangy touch of the Master Chef
is gone from my table of life.

My fare is of the greatest among humans...
But...
In losing what was shared by us – That
God's nectar is perished...
And we must dwell
separately...
here...
among the mortals............
.........forever.

An Audience

A genuine admirer I've found tonight,
Tonight.
My thoughts of shallow depth set down
She read with such delight.
And praise arose from lips so rare to
Balm my wounded ego,
Till all the past on paper there,
Was once again so regal.
I basked beneath her flood of terms,
So simple, so sincere,
And found reward for all those lines
I'd written sans a care.

To greater heights one may aspire
Who finds a soul to take
True meaning, true appraisal of
A man for his own sake.
There's not a goal too highly set
A dream too dear to dream,
When one is there to smile upon
Your efforts, as a beam
Of sunlight, seeking shining pools
Wherein your eyes do gleam.

A smile, a sneer, a grin, a tear
Contorts her youthful face –
To tell you "Ah! I see your point,
You have creative grace."

It is the end of a calm weekend. The new work week starts in the morning. I have just returned home from dinner with a friend. She is sad and fragile.

Home is a double room at the Syracuse YMCA, large enough for two roommates with two beds, two desks, and two closets, located on the third floor, overlooking the downtown scene. He is home when I get there. This will cheer me up.

He receives a phone call telling him that his Mother passed away. I drive him to the airport. I return to the large empty room on this cold, rainy, dismal night, experiencing the loneliness that comes from the sudden, unexpected departure of yet another saddened friend.

Lonely Night

Lonely night – roommate gone
Familiar traces of home – like soft touches,
Haunt with memories the surroundings.
A poor night to lose a roommate..
A poor ending for a calm weekend.

My lady friend has also been hurt.
A careless word of anger from a sibling
Has blown away the veil of courage
I had sought to build.
I'm sad
And lonely, too.

A night like this I'll fall the way of past friends
And culminate this roving age
With speeches to her, or one like her –
And we'll be one –
Then once again
I'll seek to make a home.

Retreat: a place of privacy or safety: a refuge; a place that provides shelter or protection; something to which one has recourse in difficulty.

Webster's Ninth New Collegiate Dictionary

Retreat

Far across the tropic seas,
Between two small islands dotted with sweet smelling palms,
Lies a blue and calm lagoon.

It cuddles in between the sparkling, peaceful beaches,
Rubbing gently its phosphorescent shoulders
'gainst the clean white sand.

'Neath its rippling-mirror surface,
through the cool, clear window to the deep,
appear the many silent travelers,
passing through this shaded refuge.

And on shores each side there caper
Tiny, furry creatures, fearlessly cajoling
In the warmth of sunlight,
Here, where there need be no fear.

In this place there lie my dreams,
The things I was to do,
Wished to do,
No social bounds...
No regimented thinking, breathing, doing.

In this place, calm, pure, imaginary,
Alas, too real, though never seen...
In this place...

When I go forever – and cannot come again
To visit in your castrated world...
Look for me...
There will I be...
In this place.

Each and every friend is like a unique kettle of stew.
It's hard to discern what's in it until you've made a meal of it,
and then you remain uncertain.

Roommate

A wealth of knowledge rests just here –
A roommate and a friend.
If I could know him as myself
His mystery would end.

I'd know the secrets of his soul,
The many hidden things,
That, put together, shape his life
And give his spirit wings.

No machine so complicated,
No device so incomplete,
As the human compositions
Which, each day, we chance to meet.

I would know more of his nature,
Know what secrets lie inside,
That inspire and motivate him,
Or depress and stultify.

So, my roommate, you're a challenge,
Your blueprint I would discern,
By so doing, comprehend you,
And your very nature learn.

The Middle Years

Maturation

1971 - 1978

My Mountain

Why! –
You've been around so long,
How did I miss you
All this time?

Like the mountain
Oe'rlooking my valley,
did you,
by gigantic stature alone,
seem such a formidable part
of my universe
that you went unnoticed....
all these years?

But! –
Now that I'm aware
of your presence
I am in awe...and feel
the primeval need to worship
this overpowering mystery...
that is you.

10:30 PM: Sun Valley, Idaho

The Snowball Express left from Union Station, in downtown Los Angeles, for Sun Valley, Idaho. It was filled with skiers and those who merely wanted to dress in new ski outfits while posing before a roaring fire, intermingling with beautiful people.

The package included a two way train trip, two weeks of lodging and ski lessons. Days were filled with lovely mountain scenery and exciting ski runs. Evenings were spent at dinner, drinks and dance.

The nights, for one man, were lonely.

So Far Away

What are you doing so far away?
You shouldn't leave me alone like this –
Surrounded by hundreds of happy,
joyous, celebrating people
who don't know that you are...
What I...
need.

Your breasts and
shoulders and waist and tongue and
thighs and hips and soft privacy are
born on lovely legs a thousand miles away.

Wetness and heat and breathless
moans wrenched from the pit of your
bosom...haunt my waking moments.

I am a tortured, pitiful creature of
a man...
Having you...
So far away.

Loins: the generative organs
Fruit: offspring; progeny
My children: "The fruit of my loins"

You Have Taken

You have taken the fruit of my loins
and entwined their hearts in yours,
and now, they love you.

You have taken all my bad dreams
and made a collage of bright colors,
and now, I love you.

You have taken my pulse and strength
and made it respond to yours
and now, I need you.

You have taken this man you see
and helped him feel the man he wanted to be,
and now –
and forever –
you belong to me.

All In You

When I was young I often dreamed
Of ships and seas ... and virgin shores,
Of lips and eyes .... and hot-mouthed whores.

When I was young I often planned
To build and buy ... and store up treasures,
To love and give ... in such great measures.

Now, - years have gone .... I dream much less,
There's not much time in which to press
So many dreams.

I have but few, yet deeper dreams,
So full of rich, exciting flavor,
So full of tantalizing savor.

I cannot tell just why they're better,
I am not sure just why I let her
Fill my soul.

With so few years – no more delusions,
With such short time – no more confusions
Can I afford.

Perhaps it's 'cause she's all those dreams
I'd stopped believing –
now come true.

Perhaps it's 'cause she's all those plans
I'd stopped creating –
now in view.

My virgin shore,
My hot-mouthed whore,
My stored-up treasure,
My loves great measure.
All put together,
All in one.
All in you.

Visitation

Visitation on alternate weekends.
Friday night excitement...hugs and kisses...fun activities...
quiet times...naps...meals....balloons
and toys.
Sunday evening comes too soon.
Drive them home...miles away.
Hugs and kisses....one last look
as they close the door behind them.
The sun sets over a long, black highway...and your heart.
Empty car....mournful silence...driving home alone.
On Sunday night.....again.

Sunday Night

It's midnight and I can't sleep.
Don't know why for certain,
although I know the place is void of people and voices,
beating hearts and growing things.

I know that I'm not built to be alone.
I haven't found a way to fill myself
with busy thoughts of self.

I feel a longing emptiness!
I feel a lack of feeling.
There is an uneasy, dreary, tearing sorrow inside.

I watched my children wave goodbye
and disappear into a strange house,
and I left them to drive to a place I must call home –
alone...
and I bowed my head,
filled with despair,
and I cursed my helplessness to get them back.

And I looked down a dark, straight, streaking freeway
stretching desolately into the distance,
and as each mile slipped swiftly away beneath me,
leaving them further behind
I grew more meaningless.

Oh God!
What has happened?
Where am I going?
What have I given away?
What am I getting?
Have I only questions left –
and no answers?

Oh!
How I hate Sunday night!

73

The business meetings are over.

Dinner with the customer has ended.

I sit in my room and reminisce

about someone I had met,

again,

after 20 years.

After 20 Years

I looked upon your face again,
and found it unchanged,
after all these years.

I'd asked myself where my youth
had gone – without answer.

'Til today – when I saw you –
And in your eyes – and lips
and ageless countenance,
I found the answer.....

My youth had stayed
with you.

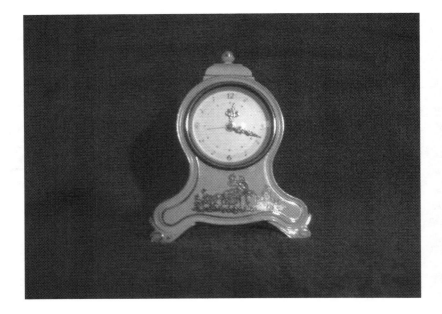

True Friendship

True friendship is more intimate
than many love affairs.

You have obligations and commitments, and loved ones.
So have I and nothing must change or touch that.

Still, I value these feelings – am
unwilling to give them up,
Will not...unless you tell me to.

I will be your friend.
Will you be mine?

You may reach out to me when you need to.
May I?

There are contracts for buying a loaf of bread,
sealing a marriage, indenturing a slave,....

How do you formalize, define, declare
a friendship?

Mostly in the eyes and heart, I think.
Gentle touches. Knowing looks. Caring.

No more heavy stuff! I promise.
Light and airy and non-threatening. OK?

Say yes, or.....
something.

I should be in bed.
Very late; very tired.

Are you pleased that I am awake,
thinking of you?

She came to spend a long weekend of adventure with me.   I was struck with the wonder of her maturation with all its young wisdom and promise. My pride of authorship changed to a realization that she was her own person, already grown far beyond my ability to shape any longer. She was my kid, but she was special.… and different…and was sailing her own course into the future.

My Kid

I was responsible for bringing her here,
for her being around.
About as responsible as nudging a stone
with your toe...

Or kissing a pretty face ...
Or blinking at a bright sun...

I really didn't do much – it was
almost nothing that I did – and
she came here.

Yet I felt responsible and I thought....
Why, if I've done this – then I must
be pretty special – and I
must know all there is to know about her –
because
I made her – and raised her -
and taught her – and so...
I must know.

But
I didn't,
Because
She, too, was very special
and different
and
unknown.

Fall

'Twas in October.
Trees were baring themselves.
Opening up stark nakedness.
Unprotected.
Knowing that Winters' onslaught
Was essential to rebirth –
In the Spring.

I came to you then.
It was our Fall, too.
Years had gone
and Fall was what was left.
I saw you there,
so beautiful and proper,
Surrounded by domesticity –
Familial things –
Sensing your nervousness with mine –
Thinking you would say hello and goodbye,
Taking your poems.....
and disappearing.

But I could not leave you – again,-
Without a sign that what we had
did not die.
If it could not live openly –
Still it must not die – but-
like the trees,
be only dormant
'til the end.

And so,
like the trees –
In the Fall of my life
I shed my leaves –
and came before you –
Bare of protective foliage.

Naked feelings
exposed to your elements,-
To tell you of my dormant
but living
love.

And leaving
I took you in my arms
to say Goodbye....
and whispered to you
"I love you.
I've always loved you.
I guess I always will..."

Then...
You responded...
so softly...
one word
that said it all.
And I knew
it lived within you, too.
Deep,
silent,
eternal,
dormant,
that might awaken –
In the Spring
of our Fall.
No more than that,-
just one word that meant
life –
to come –
again.

It was
my name.

Half A Lifetime

For almost half a lifetime – now
I've lived and wanted,
cared and dreamed,
Knowing it could never be.

For almost half a lifetime – now,
I've known the truth about my wants
and wished that "you" and "I"
were "we."

For almost half a lifetime – now
I've longed to have the chance to do
the things we could not do
'til we were free.

It's almost half a lifetime – now.
So much has happened –
So much potential –
suddenly.

'Twill soon be half a lifetime – now,
I'm filled with joy and wonder,
For, finally, I have you
and you have me.

Winter Yearning

In winter we sometimes dream
of warm days and balmy nights.
Yet here,
in winter,
is the thrill of a gentle snowflake
caught on the tongue
and tasted as chilled water.
So, too, during times of solitude
We yearn for that far companion
or lover.
Yet here,
alone,
is the joy of solitude.
The secret
is to relish today
and cherish the thrill
of anticipation.

Some Thoughts to June in January

How long will it be?
Not long, I hope.
I can keep busy, too, and time will pass.

But what a shame that we can't be
together more – to discover the treasure
in our present thing, more fully –
or build it into something grand...
or wear it out...
and then move on to other things.

Perhaps it's better this way,
Dreaming of more – not knowing.
The excitement stays high
and often unfulfilled.
But when it is – what ecstasy!

Well, then- I'll take it as it is – today,
and not look back to yesterday
except in pleasure, - and
Let tomorrow keep it's secret plan.

Today is you and me.
Today is everything.
Thank you for today.

A Love Affair

We've had an exciting thing,
Begun so slowly, innocently,
Discovering feelings,
Caring, but not daring
to let it happen.
Still, it did, and we dared, and we cared.

In another place, and another time
Your laugh and charm and wit
Would have swept my senses,
Lit my imagination,
Filled me with wanting, hoping, doing.

We have such capacity for
giving and taking with each other.
It might have been
the love story of an epoch.

Your commitments...and
My commitments...alas,
Are not the same.

You are indebted and honor your indebtedness.
I admire that, knowing that quality to be
One of the things about you I'll never forget,
And always love.

We do, now, what must be done,
Having dreamt a passionate dream
we go back now to reality,
To your life, and my life... not our life.

I hear your voice still...in the dark,
Softly telling me of your resolution,

An unspoken plea hidden deep within.
A plea I cannot answer.

You'll go your way now, carrying a memory,
A bitter-sweet recall over your remaining years,
Knowing with certainty that I, too,
Hold in my heart that same poignant photograph.

Your relationship with them will grow from this.
I'll be better for it, too, standing tall and proud,
Knowing this is best for you and yours.
I am stronger than before, thanks to you.

So- go now, fulfill your obligation to them,
As I fulfill mine to you...
By letting go...
of your hand.

The Later Years

Reality & Whimsy

1997 – 2010

The Miracle

When I look around me for something
enduring, dependable, comforting –
I find my Mother gone; my Father,
full of love, yet needing more than me,
My children entering their own lives –
And you – so far away – your love
available all these years – now at
a price so dear to me, and to you,
that it doesn't seem we can make it happen.

Yet, as I look around, your love is prominent,
a thing that was never far away –
That I've always known and cherished
and wanted
and dreamed about.

I reach out and touch you; secretly, as
worshippers touched Jesus robe, hoping not to
disturb the procession of life, yet knowing
the blessing and joy of that stolen touch.

You are to me that miracle of healing
and rejoicing that wandered through
my village and, passing through my life,
changed it,
forever.

Expect A Miracle

Sometimes things seem to overwhelm me,
I look into the mirror and see someone old
and many of my dreams yet unfulfilled.
I worry that there are fewer years left than I have already spent,
and my agenda is still long.
And somewhere comes the echo of past friends saying
"whattaya expect, a miracle?"

Sometimes I have aches and pains
That come like thieves in the night
and cause parts of my body to betray me.
Worse are the times the pain comes from my mind
and I can't sleep
and I agonize about the things I can't control
and wish I could
and I hear again,
"whattaya expect, a miracle?"

Worst of all
I think of the mistakes I made
the decisions I wish I could undo
the losses that can't be recovered,
and yearn to make it all right again...
and it whispers
"whattaya expect, a Miracle?"

And then this time of year comes
and I see the end of one year and the beginning of another
a new beginning..
and I think of all the things that have new beginnings
despite the dark nights and cold days
trees, flowers, babies, lovers
and I say, "why not?"

HE promised it to us,
why not?
So I say to you...
"Expect a Miracle"
I do.

No Miracles

I've been a fortress all my life,
Enduring countless onslaughts,
Rigid, proud, strong, resilient.
In the face of everything that came
I remained determined and full of hope,
always hope,
Never ending, never faltering, never capitulating,
Hope.

Each blow,
though sometimes driving me to my knees,
was answered by standing tall again,
Gazing straight ahead and swearing to survive.
Spurred on by the belief that by perseverance,
things would get better.
There remained, always,
Hope

One day, not too long ago,
The unthinkable occurred.
After that, no rationale existed for Hope.....
I struggled up once more.
I reached deep inside
And decided to expect...yet again..
a Miracle.

I marched ahead declaring
My expectation.
I expect a miracle!
I shouted.
So should you!
I cried to the world.
As if, by convincingly declaring it,
it would come true.

But it didn't.

It is that time of year again....
and I know, now.
Now I can answer those ghostly voices from my youth
which still derisively echo, over and over,
"Whattaya expect, a Miracle?"

No, my dear, departed, boyhood friends,
No.
Not anymore.
There are no miracles left.
There are no Miracles.

Except the little ones I find now and then,
When I can sit in a rocking chair,
and relish the pure, unconditional love of the little ones.
Those are my miracles now.

Spring Rain

You came so unexpectedly,
Much like a warm Spring rain,
A dormant bud, within me,
Awoke to your refrain.

It flourished and grew quickly,
As flowers often do.
It's new life flowing, glowing,
Here, inside me, too.

I nurture it so gently,
To postpone its sure demise,
A bruise, a careless touching,
Would, I know, not be too wise.

Its life, like all, is finite,
This flower soon must die,
Dropping petals, one by one,
Until it lifeless lies.

"Til all that's left is memory
Of its sweet, gentle caress,
And the soft, yet haunting scent
Of a short-lived happiness.

And I will visit often,
That memory so clear,
And be happy that a flower,
Of such beauty,
once lived here.

The Dance

The night was not unusual
Except that you were there.
Small talk, hello to old friends,
Introduction to new people,
Introduction to you.

Music playing indoors
drifted out to the balcony.
Wandering inside I danced
with others.
You did too.

A mutual friend
pressed your hand into mine.
Commanded us
to be together,
to dance.

With casual pleasure
we touched,
moved to the rhythms
of the music,
and our thoughts.

Music ended.
People drifted to the doors,
You out one,
I another.

Clutched in my hand,
a scrap of paper
with a number
That held a promise.

Awakening

I met you,
Without Striving,
With such ease,
So simply.

My heart had slept for so long
That it awoke slowly,
Pulsing softly -
at first.

Then,
with increasing tempo,
All of me awoke,
to you
and life
again.

Valentine

I tried to find a valentine
with what I want to say,
But one that used such harmless words
You'd not be scared away.

I read the "God, I love you so..."
and "Cause you are so great..."
And "I can't live without ya..."
And "We were meant by fate!"

And concluded none of these were right,
They even scared me, too.
I needed one to rhyme with words
Like "fun" and "me" and "you."

So I gave up on Hallmark
and their cloying, sucrose fashion,
and taking pen in hand set out
to say it with less passion.

You are cute and smart and funny,
stunning and sexy, too.
Shocking, open, honest.
I feel good with you.

Hope that as time passes by
you'll feel the very same way,
And we'll become tight buddies,
A "couple," as they say.

So, please grant me now this favor,
Make my life sublime,
Tell me that you like me
And you'll be my Valentine!

"Ken and Mary are celebrating their umpteenth wedding anniversary. Can you write something for them?"

"I don't know them very well. Can you tell me more about them? Stuff I can use?"

"Mary was born in Danbury, Illinois. She was a Delta Airlines stewardess when she met Ken, a businessman. There is lots more I can tell you, but strictly off the record......(psst....psst... psst)."

"Gee, that's good stuff. Let me think about it and I'll give it a shot."

Happy Anni-ver-sary

I met a couple people,
Not too long ago.
I must say that I liked them,
Right from the old "get-go."

Still don't know them very well,
But I'm learning as I go,
That they're the kind of people
Most people like to know.

She was a simple country girl
When she began to fly.
He was a blooming businessman,
When first she caught his eye.

I guess it wasn't very long
Before they tied the knot.
I've heard that their relationship
Was really kinda Hot!

Well, years have passed and though they've had
The usual Ups and Downs,
They've stuck it out, They've smiled along,
And minimized the frowns.

I s'pose it could be booze or drugs,
Or great religious zeal.
Or maybe, after all these years
They still find sex appeal.

In any case it's clear to me,
And anyone who looks,
That they're still a lovin' couple,
Like in those pulpy paper books.

Now, I had to stretch to get a rhyme
for a town that ends with "bury."
So here comes poetic license
That is extra-ordinary.

Now here's a toast to good old Ken
and Mary from Danbury.
May you have a joyous, loving day
This Anni -ver-sary.

"Church services were a mandatory event…three times a week for the whole family. Sunday morning was the main course followed by Tuesday evening prayer meeting. On Thursday another full service was held in hopes it would tide us over until the next Sunday. These were full bodied events lasting two hours or more."

"During those long hours … I learned how to hold my breath for over three minutes, gasping for air at the end with a stifled sound that caused the nearest sitting parishioners to look around curiously. I also learned how to hold other things for a long time because the only bathroom ……. was through a door up in front, on the right hand side of the altar."

"That is, no doubt, where I developed an intense dislike for long meetings, a feeling that carried over to adulthood."

Joseph N. Manfredo: *Only The Living*

The Board Meeting

I sat in a board meeting,
It ran 'til very late.
'Cause every person in the room
Chose to pontificate.

They talked 'til the wee hours.
Each one said something smart.
And yet, when it was over,
We landed at the start.

Now I don't mind the time we spent,
I had a drink or two.
But if you sat there sober,
Gosh! I really pitied you.

You listened to the rhetoric,
The pros and all the cons.
You struggled to evaluate
The merits of each one.

And when the night was over
You staggered out the door
And wondered, really, after all,
Just what was all this for?

The Yacht Club Board has done its thing,
It's duties sure to keep.
And all attendees have a month
To catch up on their sleep.

So here's to all you Commodores
And you Board members, too.
We gripe and fuss, yet we all know
That we depend on you.

Our thanks for all the painful hours
You spend on our behalf.
We love, admire and honor you,
Respectfully......................your Staff.

The second floor rear apartment had windows that looked out onto the roof of the building below. It was black tarred and sloped downward from all edges to the center of the roof where a small, grated drain hole sat. In Summer it reflected sunlight and provided heat that dried the clothes hung above it on a clothesline. In Winter it was covered with frigid snow.

During the rainy season it was a fascinating pallet of rushing, swirling water that swept in ever tightening circles toward the center of the rooftop and, with a gurgling, slurping noise plunged down into the grated drain. While black clouds loomed overhead, lightening cracked the sky and reflected in the twisting torrent.

A young boy, watching this panorama of nature, was mesmerized and awestruck by the spectacle. Years later, during a thunderstorm, memories came flooding back.

Thunder Shower

Sweet rain. Gurgle and splash – child of Heaven-
Little droplets make shiny puddles beneath a moonlit night.
Thunder overhead....
the distance lending a haunting dullness to the sound –
And romantic bloods move faster in veins.
Silent night, serenaded by the song of rainfall
And like all else, enchanted, mysterious and lovely.

Through all this loneliness comes, yet a happy loneliness –
Rather sweet, if painful.
Better nights I have not known,
though better company has been mine.
The hour approaches and passes and night grows deeper
To creep closer to dawn
And farther from sleep.

Nights such as this are meant for wakeful ears and soft thoughts.
Beauty, in its blackest veil,
holds a fascinating view.
My heart strikes time with the sporadic "bloop"
of droplets upon the roof,
outside my window.

And I find tranquility here.
My thoughts flow freely, effortlessly,
As the breath comes leisurely
After a heavy thunder storm.

I doubt I shall ever hear
A sound more meaningful,
Nor one that stirs the imagination
And slumbering dreams of the soul,
Than that long, low, rumble of "Thor's" hammer
after the first, piercing repercussion.

This, to me, is magic
And I lie awake in bed –
A child,
Fascinated by this play-thing
From the great upstairs.

An invitation!

"Repondez s'il vous plait!"

It reads:

"Wedding Reception, 4 PM sharp!
No Gifts.
RSVP no later than April 10th."

How to repondez?

A poem!

RSVP

We are honored that you've asked us
To share your big event.
I hope we've beat the deadline
which you set for April 10th.

We did have several conflicts,
other plans so hard to change,
It caused us consternation,
how would we rearrange?

I called our stalwart President
and told him, Sorry Bush!
We're canceling the meeting.
We cannot save your "tush."

And then the Queen got flustered when
we called across the Sea
To postpone the Knighthood
which she'd hoped
to give Jo Ann and me.

Martha Stewart was the hardest,
she was hurt by our decision
To skip her first TV show
since getting out of Prison.

So, Yes, we both will be there
on the day you tie that knot.
Sans gift,
just us,
with lots of love,
4 PM on the dot!

In 2005 the major grocery stores in
California went out on strike.

Picket lines, with waving signs, confronted shoppers.

Shopping and planning for the Thanksgiving
holiday became a challenge.

The time was ripe for a unique Thanksgiving card.

A Thanksgiving Wish

So many things to think about,
To be so thankful for,
So many things to wish for you,
Well here's a couple more.

May all your Turkey shopping
Be free of toil and stress,
May crossing grocery picket lines
Be done without duress.

May all your Turkey, stuffing too,
And pies and creams and gin.
Be absolutely calorie free,
And tasting oh, so thin!

When your guests have finally gone,
And the festive day's a wrap,
May all your dishes clean themselves,
So you can take a nap

When Friday morning rolls around,
And all the food is in you,
May your bathroom scale tell one more lie,
And show a brand new THIN you.

The Missing Child

I do not know where you have gone,
I know not where you may
Have sought comfort and refuge
On this, your special day.

Once you were small, not long ago,
Why you were just knee high,
And everything was fun and joy
Between us, you and I.

Childhood and the teenage years
Are only memories now.
You managed to grow up so soon,
And slipped away somehow.

I wonder if, at last, you rest
and if you ever yearn
For shadows of the distant past
And wish you could return?

Do you miss me, I'd like to know,
With sorrow, love and pain,
As I miss you and long to see
You close, just once again.

Especially heavy lies my heart
On this auspicious day,
This anniversary of your birth,
That finds you far away.

Happy Birthday, missing child,
May this next year bring new
And healing blessings, on their way,
With love, from me, to you.

Gettin' Old

I look in the mirror
and say a prayer
Of thanks to the Gods
that my face is still there.

My locks are much thinner
My face is less fair.
Glad I've lived long enough
to lose my hair.

Dying young, while good lookin',
Ain't a bargain to me.
Livin' long, causin' trouble,
That's where I want to be.

So I'll linger a while longer
Kinda' messin' with you.
When I finally depart
You'll be glad....I will too!

Sayin' goodbye ain't easy, so I won't.
I 'spect we'll meet up again real soon.
Meanwhile....
you take care.

About The Author

Born in Utica, New York this son of immigrant Italian parents inherited a love of music, art and the beauty of the written word. He holds a Bachelor of Mechanical Engineering degree from Kettering University and a Master of Science in Business Administration from California State University, Northridge. He is currently retired and living in Southern California.